The Calling and Greatness of John the Baptist

Joshua Rhoades

Published by Joshua Paul Rhoades, 2024.

THE CALLING AND GREATNESS OF JOHN THE BAPTIST

First edition. September 29, 2024.

Copyright © 2024 Joshua Rhoades.

ISBN: 979-8227199119

Written by Joshua Rhoades.

Also by Joshua Rhoades

Courage Under Fire: David's Stand On The Battlefield
Jonah's Journey: Voices Of Redemption And Lessons In Obedience
The Furnace Of Faith: 12 Principles From The Heat Of Faith
Whispers of Hope: Inspiring Stories of Men's Prayers In Scripture
Frontier Legends: The Oregon Dream
Elijah: A Beacon Of Boldness
HOOK, LINE & SAVIOUR - Faith Reflections from Fishing
Driven By Faith: Motor Racing Inspired Christian Life
30 Day Devotional - Bold and Strong- Coffee Devotions for a Courageous
Christian Walk
Authentic Christianity: The Heart of Old Time Religion
Consider The Ant - God's Tiny Preachers
Flee Fornication: The Plea For Purity
Renewed Hope- How to Find Encouragement in God
Sounding The Call - The Voice of Conviction
The Altar - Where Heaven Meets Earth
The Bible's Battlefields- Timeless Lessons from Ancient Wars
The Sacred Art of Silence - How Silence Speaks in Scripture
Under Fire- The Sanctity of the Traditional Biblical Home
Who Is on the Lord's Side? A Call to Righteousness
What Is Truth? - From Skepticism to Submission
First and Goal- Faith and Football Fundamentals
From Dugout to Devotion- Spiritual Lessons from Baseball
Par for the Course- Faith and Fairways
The Believer's Pace- Tools for Running Life's Marathon
The Immutable Fortress- Security in God's Unchanging Nature
Biblical Bravery
Deer Stands and Devotions: A Hunter's Walk with God

Dedication

To you, dear reader, who holds this book in your hands, I want to begin by thanking you for choosing to journey through the life of one of the greatest figures in Scripture—John the Baptist. As you look into his story, I hope you will be stirred, challenged, and ultimately transformed by the remarkable lessons his life offers us today.

John the Baptist was a man like no other, a beacon of unwavering faith, a fearless voice crying out in the wilderness, preparing the way for the Savior. His life was not marked by fame, wealth, or worldly success. Instead, his greatness was found in his complete surrender to God's will, his relentless passion for truth, and his unwavering commitment to pointing others to Christ. In a world filled with distractions and countless voices calling us in different directions, John stood firm. He preached repentance without compromise, confronted sin without fear, and lived his life for a purpose greater than himself. John's singular mission was to lead people to Jesus, and in that, we find the heart of this book's message—pointing everyone to Christ, as John the Baptist did.

I dedicate this book to you with a plea: may you be deeply encouraged to live your life with the same sense of purpose and urgency as John the Baptist. Today, we are surrounded by a world that is lost and searching for hope, truth, and salvation. Many are wandering through a spiritual wilderness, not knowing where to turn. You, like John, have a calling—a calling to be a voice in this wilderness, pointing people to the only One who can save them: Jesus Christ. Just as John proclaimed, "He must increase, but I must decrease," we too are called to diminish ourselves so that Christ might be seen in us. In every conversation, every action, and every moment of our lives, we have the opportunity to point others to the Savior.

As you read through the pages of this book, you will see John's relentless courage, even in the face of persecution. He did not shy away from hard truths, nor did he seek personal comfort or glory. His eyes were fixed solely on God's purpose for his life. What would it look like for you to live with that same conviction today? Imagine the impact you could have if you allowed your voice to be one that calls others to repentance, that leads others to Christ, even when it's uncomfortable, even when it's costly.

This book is more than a biography—it is a challenge. A challenge to live for something greater than ourselves, to embrace the humility of John the Baptist, and to make Christ known in all we do. It is a reminder that, in a world that desperately needs hope, we are called to be the light that points others to the true Light of the world.

Dear reader, I pray that this book moves you to action. May John's life of faith, courage, and selfless devotion to Christ inspire you to live with boldness and purpose. And most importantly, may it encourage you to point everyone you encounter to the one and only Savior, Jesus Christ. For as John the Baptist showed us, there is no greater calling, no greater mission, and no greater privilege than to make Christ known. This is my hope for you as you turn these pages, that you will be strengthened, inspired, and forever changed by the lessons you will learn from the life of God's chosen herald.

Introduction

"God's Chosen Herald - The Calling and Greatness of John the Baptist" explores the remarkable life of a man divinely appointed to prepare the way for the Saviour, Jesus Christ. John the Baptist's life was marked by unwavering faith, boldness, and deep humility. From his miraculous birth to his martyrdom, John's greatness was not in worldly success but in his absolute obedience to God's will. Called to be a prophet in the wilderness, he preached repentance with fiery conviction, fearlessly confronting sin in all ranks, from commoners to kings. John's singular mission was to point others to Christ, and he did so with humility, famously declaring, "He must increase, but I must decrease." His entire life demonstrated selfless devotion, as he refused to seek personal glory, focusing only on fulfilling God's plan. Even when misunderstood by his followers, persecuted by religious leaders, and imprisoned for speaking truth, John remained steadfast in his calling. The book peers into how John's resolute courage and dedication to God's truth ultimately led to his martyrdom, cementing his place as a pivotal figure in God's redemptive plan. Through the lens of Scripture, "God's Chosen Herald – The Calling and Greatness of John the Baptist" illuminates how John's calling and greatness continue to inspire Christians to live boldly, faithfully, and humbly, pointing to Christ as the only source of salvation and ultimate truth.

Chapter 1 - Messenger of the Messiah

John the Baptist was a remarkable figure in the Bible, and what made him great is especially emphasized in his role as the Messenger of the Messiah. He was chosen by God to be the forerunner of Christ, the one who would announce the coming of the Savior. This role was not just important; it was crucial to the unfolding of God's plan of salvation for the world. John's entire life was dedicated to this mission, and he embraced it with a boldness and humility that truly set him apart. From his birth, John was marked as special. His parents, Zechariah and Elizabeth, were righteous before God but had no children. In their old age, an angel appeared to Zechariah and announced that they would have a son, and his name would be John. Even before he was born, it was clear that John was going to have a significant role in God's plan. He would be filled with the Holy Spirit even from his mother's womb, and his mission would be to prepare the way for the coming of the Lord. This was a monumental task, as John was the one who would call people to repentance and get their hearts ready for Jesus. John's greatness can also be seen in the way he faithfully fulfilled this calling. He didn't shy away from his mission, and he didn't let fear or doubt stop him from proclaiming the message God had given him. John went out into the wilderness, away from the comforts of life, to preach a message of repentance. He wore clothes made of camel's hair and ate locusts and wild honey, showing that he wasn't concerned with material things. His focus was entirely on the task God had given him. John's message was simple but powerful: "Repent ye: for the kingdom of heaven is at hand" (Matthew 3:2). He knew that the Messiah was coming soon, and he wanted the people to be ready. John wasn't afraid to speak the truth, even when it was difficult or unpopular. He called out sin wherever he saw it, whether it was among the religious leaders of the time or in the lives of ordinary people. John's boldness in confronting sin and calling people to turn back to God was one of the things that made him so great. He wasn't concerned about what people thought of him; he was only concerned about being faithful to God and fulfilling the mission he had been given. Another key aspect of John's greatness was his humility. Even though he had a large following and many people came to hear him preach, he never sought fame or glory for himself. In fact, John was always careful to point people to Jesus. He made it clear that he was not the Messiah, but rather the one sent to prepare the way for Him. When Jesus began His public ministry, some of John's disciples were concerned that people were now going to Jesus instead of John. But John wasn't upset by this. He knew that this was the way it was supposed to be. John said, "He must increase, but I must decrease" (John 3:30). This statement shows John's deep understanding of his role in God's plan and his willingness to step aside so that Jesus could take the spotlight. John's humility is a key part of what made him great because it showed that he was focused on God's glory, not his own. John's greatness was also seen in the way he fulfilled the prophecies about him. The Old Testament prophets had spoken about a messenger who would come to prepare the way for the Lord. In Isaiah 40:3, it says, "The voice of him that crieth in the wilderness, Prepare ye the way of the LORD, make straight in the desert a highway for our God". John the Baptist was the fulfillment of this prophecy. He was the voice crying in the wilderness, calling people to prepare their hearts for the coming of the Messiah. In Malachi 3:1, it says, "Behold, I will send my messenger, and he shall prepare the way before me". Jesus Himself confirmed that John was the fulfillment of these prophecies when He said, "This is he, of whom it is written, Behold, I send my messenger before thy face, which shall prepare thy way before thee" (Matthew 11:10). By fulfilling these prophecies, John played a critical role in God's plan of redemption. But John's greatness wasn't just about his mission or the prophecies he fulfilled. It was also about his character and his faithfulness to God. John was willing to stand up for righteousness, even when it was dangerous to do so. He boldly confronted King Herod for his sinful behavior, specifically for taking his brother's wife, Herodias, as his own. This confrontation eventually led to John's imprisonment and death. Herodias held a grudge against John and used her daughter to manipulate Herod into having John beheaded. Even in the face of such danger, John remained faithful to God and continued to speak the truth. His courage in the face of persecution and his willingness to die for what was right is another reason why John the Baptist was great. Jesus recognized John's greatness not just because of his ministry, but also because of his place in the grand narrative of God's plan. John was the last and greatest of the prophets who came before Jesus. His ministry marked the end of the old covenant and the beginning of the new one. Jesus said, "For all the prophets and the law prophesied until John" (Matthew 11:13). John's ministry was the final step in preparing the world for the coming of the Messiah. He was the bridge between the Old Testament and the New Testament, and his role was critical in the unfolding of God's plan of salvation. However, Jesus also made a surprising statement in Matthew 11:11. After praising John's greatness, Jesus said, "Notwithstanding he that is least in the kingdom of heaven is greater than he". This statement reveals an important truth about greatness in God's kingdom. While John was the greatest of those born under the old covenant, Jesus was introducing a new covenant. In this new covenant, greatness is not measured by worldly standards, but by one's relationship with Christ. Even the least in the kingdom of heaven—those who have been born again through faith in Jesus—are considered greater than John because they have experienced the fullness of God's grace and the indwelling of the Holy Spirit. This doesn't diminish John's greatness, but it points to the even greater reality of the new life that Jesus offers to all who believe in Him. In conclusion, what made John the Baptist great according to the Bible was his unique role as the Messenger of the Messiah. John was chosen by God to prepare the way for Jesus, and he faithfully fulfilled this mission. He preached a powerful message of repentance, called people to turn back to God, and pointed them to Jesus. John's boldness in confronting sin, his humility in stepping aside for Jesus, and his willingness to die for righteousness are all key aspects of his greatness. Additionally, John fulfilled the prophecies about him, serving as the bridge between the old and new covenants. Jesus Himself praised John's greatness, but also pointed to the even greater reality of the kingdom of heaven. John the Baptist stands as a powerful example of what it means to live a life fully dedicated to God's purposes, and his legacy continues to inspire believers today.

Chapter 2 - Mission of Repentance

John the Baptist's greatness is deeply connected to his mission of repentance, a powerful message that prepared the hearts of the people for the coming of the Kingdom of Heaven. John's message of repentance is central to his ministry and plays a vital role in God's plan of salvation. John's life and ministry were focused on calling people to turn away from their sins and return to God. His message wasn't easy or soft; it was direct, urgent, and often challenging, but it was exactly what the people needed to hear at that time. John knew that repentance was necessary for the people to truly receive the message of the Messiah, Jesus Christ. This message wasn't just about changing behavior—it was about a deep, internal transformation that could only come from a sincere heart. When we look at John's role in the context of the Bible, we see that he was specifically chosen by God for this purpose. The angel Gabriel foretold John's birth to his father, Zechariah, explaining that John would "turn many of the children of Israel to the Lord their God" (Luke 1:16). This was John's mission from the very beginning: to call people back to God through repentance. He was born for this purpose, and he fulfilled it with incredible faithfulness and dedication. John's message of repentance was not new in one sense, as the prophets of the Old Testament had also called the people of Israel to repent. However, John's message was unique in that it came at a critical time in history—just before the coming of Jesus, the Savior of the world. The Bible says that John was "the voice of one crying in the wilderness, Prepare ye the way of the Lord, make his paths straight" (Matthew 3:3). This was a fulfillment of the prophecy in Isaiah 40:3, where it was foretold that a messenger would come to prepare the way for the Lord. John's role as this messenger was to prepare the people's hearts through repentance so that they would be ready to receive Jesus and the message of the Kingdom of Heaven. John the Baptist preached in the wilderness of Judea, far from the religious centers of power like Jerusalem. This is significant because it shows that John's message wasn't about gaining popularity or aligning with the religious elite. Instead, his message was meant for everyone, from the common people to the religious leaders, and he wasn't afraid to call out sin no matter where he found it. John's ministry in the wilderness also symbolized a break from the corruption and hypocrisy that had infiltrated the religious institutions of the day. He called people out of their comfort zones, both physically and spiritually, urging them to leave behind their sins and return to God with sincere hearts. John's message of repentance wasn't just a call for the people to confess their sins; it was a call to a complete change of heart and mind. The word "repent" means to turn around or change direction. In a spiritual sense, it means turning away from sin and turning toward God. John made it clear that repentance wasn't just about saying the right words or performing religious rituals. It was about true, heartfelt change. John challenged the people to examine their lives and their hearts, to see if they were truly living in a way that honored God. He warned them that simply being descendants of Abraham wasn't enough to save them. "And think not to say within yourselves, We have Abraham to our father: for I say unto you, that God is able of these stones to raise up children unto Abraham" (Matthew 3:9). John's message was a wake-up call, reminding the people that their heritage and religious practices couldn't save them if their hearts were not right with God. This focus on genuine repentance is one of the things that made John's ministry so powerful and effective. John also used the powerful imagery of baptism as part of his message of repentance. In the Bible, baptism symbolizes cleansing and renewal, and for John, it represented a public declaration of repentance. Those who came to be baptized by John were making a public commitment to turn away from their sins and live in a way that was pleasing to God. John's baptism was not the same as the Christian baptism that would come later, but it was a symbol of the people's desire to be cleansed from their sins and prepared for the coming of the Messiah. John understood that true repentance required more than just words—it required action. That's why he told the people, "Bring forth therefore fruits meet for repentance" (Matthew 3:8). In other words, repentance should be accompanied by a change in behavior. It wasn't enough to say you were sorry for your sins; you had to demonstrate that repentance through your actions. John challenged the people to live lives that reflected their repentance, to show through their deeds that they had truly turned back to God. One of the most remarkable aspects of John's ministry was his boldness. He didn't hold back in calling out sin, even when it put him in danger. He preached repentance to everyone, from the Pharisees and Sadducees, the religious leaders of the day, to King Herod himself. John wasn't afraid to confront the hypocrisy and corruption he saw in the religious and political leaders, and he did so with courage and conviction. When the Pharisees and Sadducees came to observe John's baptisms, he didn't welcome them with open arms. Instead, he rebuked them, calling them a "generation of vipers" and warning them of the coming judgment if they did not repent (Matthew 3:7). John's willingness to speak the truth, no matter the cost, is one of the things that made him so great. Even when his message put him in direct conflict with the powerful people of his day, he remained faithful to his mission. John's confrontation with King Herod over Herod's unlawful marriage to his brother's wife, Herodias, is a powerful example of his commitment to truth and righteousness. John publicly condemned Herod's actions, knowing full well that it could lead to his imprisonment or worse. And indeed, John was arrested and eventually executed because of his stand for righteousness. Despite the danger, John remained faithful to his mission of calling people to repentance. He never compromised his message, even when it cost him his freedom and ultimately his life. John's unwavering commitment to his mission is a testament to his greatness. Another aspect of John's greatness was his humility. Despite the crowds that came to hear him preach and the respect he commanded from the people, John never sought to glorify himself. He always pointed people to Jesus. John knew that his role was to prepare the way for the Messiah, not to be the Messiah himself. When people asked him if he was the Christ, John made it clear that he was not. He said, "I indeed baptize you with water unto repentance: but he that cometh after me is mightier than I, whose shoes I am not worthy to bear" (Matthew 3:11). John understood his place in God's plan, and he embraced it with humility. He knew that his mission was not about building his own reputation but about preparing the way for Jesus. When Jesus began His public ministry and people started to follow Him instead of John, John's disciples were concerned. But John wasn't worried. He understood that his mission had been to prepare the people for Jesus, and now that Jesus was here, John was content to step back. He said, "He must increase, but I must decrease" (John 3:30). This statement is a powerful example of John's humility and his understanding of his role in God's plan. John's greatness was not in seeking his own glory but in faithfully carrying out the mission God had given him. John the Baptist's mission of repentance was not only about preparing people for the first coming of Jesus but also about preparing them for the Kingdom of Heaven. His message was a call to turn away from sin and turn toward God, to live lives that were pleasing to God and reflected true repentance. John understood that repentance was necessary for the people to be ready to receive the message of Jesus and to enter into the Kingdom of Heaven. He preached with urgency, knowing that the time was short and that the Messiah was coming soon. John's message of repentance is still relevant today. Just as the people in John's time needed to turn away from their sins and prepare their hearts for the coming of Jesus, we too need to repent and turn back to God. John's call to repentance reminds us that we cannot enter the Kingdom of Heaven on our own terms. We must humble ourselves, confess our sins, and seek God's forgiveness. John the Baptist's mission of repentance was a critical part of God's plan of salvation. His boldness in proclaiming the truth, his unwavering commitment to his mission, and his humility in pointing people to Jesus are all aspects of what made him great. John understood that repentance was necessary for the people to be ready for the coming of the Kingdom of Heaven, and he faithfully carried out his mission, even when it put him in danger. His message of repentance prepared the hearts of the people for the coming of Jesus, and his example continues to inspire us to live lives of true repentance and faithfulness to God.

Chapter 3 - Marked by Humility

John the Baptist was truly marked by humility, and this is one of the most significant aspects of what made him great. His entire life and ministry centered around preparing the way for Jesus Christ, the Messiah, and in doing so, he displayed an extraordinary level of humility that set him apart from others. John's role in God's plan was remarkable from the beginning, yet he never sought to glorify himself. His mission was clear: to point people toward Jesus, not to draw attention to himself. In John 3:30, he famously said, "He must increase, but I must decrease," which perfectly captures his humble heart and deep understanding of his purpose in relation to Christ. John's humility is first evident in how he lived his life. Unlike many religious leaders of his time, John didn't seek power, wealth, or recognition. He lived a simple life in the wilderness, wearing clothing made of camel's hair and eating locusts and wild honey (Matthew 3:4). His choice of lifestyle reflected his commitment to his calling and his rejection of worldly comforts or praise. John wasn't concerned with the trappings of fame or fortune; he was focused on fulfilling the mission God had given him, which was to prepare the people for the coming of Jesus. In this way, his humility shone through in his actions and choices, showing that his priority was God's plan, not his own advancement. When people came to John, drawn by his powerful message of repentance and his bold preaching, he consistently pointed them toward Jesus. He had a large following, and many people considered him a great prophet. But John never allowed this attention to inflate his ego or make him lose sight of his role. He knew that his greatness wasn't about his own ability or influence, but about the One he was sent to prepare the way for. John was always clear that his role was secondary to Jesus. In John 1:27, he said, "He it is, who coming after me is preferred before me, whose shoe's latchet I am not worthy to unloose." This statement reveals the depth of John's humility. In the cultural context of that time, untying someone's sandals was considered a task for the lowest of servants, yet John said he wasn't even worthy to perform this humble act for Jesus. Despite the respect and admiration he received from the people, John understood that his worth and significance were nothing compared to the glory and majesty of Jesus Christ. John's humility was further highlighted when people began to wonder if he might be the Messiah. In Luke 3:15-16, it says, "And as the people were in expectation, and all men mused in their hearts of John, whether he were the Christ, or not; John answered, saying unto them all, I indeed baptize you with water; but one mightier than I cometh, the latchet of whose shoes I am not worthy to unloose." John didn't hesitate to correct their misunderstanding. He didn't take advantage of their confusion or try to claim more authority than was rightfully his. Instead, he made it clear that his role was to point the way to the One who was far greater. John knew that he was just the messenger, and his mission was to prepare people's hearts for the true Savior. This willingness to step aside and give Jesus the spotlight is a profound example of John's humility. He understood that the purpose of his ministry was not to gain followers for himself, but to lead people to Christ. This is especially evident when some of John's disciples came to him, concerned that people were starting to follow Jesus instead of him. In John 3:26-30, they said, "Rabbi, he that was with thee beyond Jordan, to whom thou barest witness, behold, the same baptizeth, and all men come to him." But John wasn't bothered by this at all. In fact, he rejoiced in it. He replied, "A man can receive nothing, except it be given him from heaven. Ye yourselves bear me witness, that I said, I am not the Christ, but that I am sent before him. He that hath the bride is the bridegroom: but the friend of the bridegroom, which standeth and heareth him, rejoiceth greatly because of the bridegroom's voice: this my joy therefore is fulfilled. He must increase, but I must decrease." John's response shows just how deeply rooted his humility was. He compared himself to the friend of the bridegroom, whose joy comes from seeing the bridegroom receive honor and attention. In this analogy, John saw himself as the friend, and Jesus as the bridegroom. John's greatest joy came not from his own success or recognition, but from seeing Jesus honored and exalted. His humility allowed him to take joy in decreasing so that Jesus could increase. This mindset is what made John the Baptist truly great in the eyes of God. His greatness wasn't about his own accomplishments or how many followers he had. It was about his willingness to step back and let Jesus take center stage. John's humility also helped him fulfill his role as the forerunner of Christ in a unique and powerful way. His message of repentance was bold and uncompromising, and he didn't shy away from confronting sin, even in the lives of powerful people like King Herod. But at the same time, John never sought to elevate himself or his own authority. He always made it clear that his authority came from God, and his message was about preparing the way for someone far greater than himself. This balance of boldness and humility is rare, and it made John's ministry incredibly effective. People listened to John because they could see that he wasn't promoting himself or seeking his own glory. He was sincerely focused on fulfilling the mission God had given him. Even in the face of danger and opposition, John's humility remained evident. When John was imprisoned by King Herod for speaking out against Herod's unlawful marriage to his brother's wife, he didn't waver in his commitment to the truth or in his dedication to his calling. He continued to trust in God's plan, even though it led to his imprisonment and eventual death. John's humility was not weakness; it was strength. He didn't cling to his own safety or reputation, but instead remained faithful to his mission, trusting that God's plan was greater than his own personal circumstances. Another aspect of John's humility was his willingness to ask questions and seek confirmation, even in moments of doubt. While John was in prison, he sent some of his disciples to ask Jesus, "Art thou he that should come, or do we look for another?" (Matthew 11:3). This question reveals that even someone as great as John the Baptist had moments of uncertainty. But instead of letting pride stop him from seeking answers, John humbly sought confirmation from Jesus. He wasn't afraid to acknowledge his doubts and look to Christ for reassurance. Jesus' response to John's disciples was to point to the miracles He was performing as evidence of His identity as the Messiah, and then He said something remarkable about John: "Verily I say unto you, Among them that are born of women there hath not risen a greater than John the Baptist: notwithstanding he that is least in the kingdom of heaven is greater than he" (Matthew 11:11). Jesus affirmed John's greatness, not because of his power or influence, but because of his faithfulness and humility in carrying out the role he had been given. John's humility in acknowledging Christ's supremacy and his willingness to decrease so that Jesus could increase is the heart of what made him great. He understood that his life and ministry were not about him, but about preparing the way for the One who would bring salvation to the world. John's humility was a reflection of his deep understanding of God's plan and his place within it. He didn't seek to build his own legacy or gain recognition for himself. Instead, he devoted his life to pointing people to Jesus and preparing their hearts to receive the Messiah. In today's world, where self-promotion and personal achievement are often prioritized, John's humility stands as a powerful example of what true greatness looks like in God's eyes. John's greatness was not in his own accomplishments, but in his willingness to be a vessel for God's work, to point others to Christ, and to step aside when the time came for Jesus to take center stage. This is a lesson that we can all learn from. True greatness is not about how much we accomplish or how much recognition we receive. It's about our willingness to humble ourselves before God, to serve others, and to point people to Jesus rather than seeking our own glory. John the Baptist's life was marked by humility, and this is what made him great. His understanding of his role in relation to Christ, his joy in seeing Jesus exalted, and his willingness to decrease so that Jesus could increase are all powerful examples of the kind of humility that God values. John's life and ministry remind us that true greatness comes from serving God faithfully, even when it means stepping aside and letting someone else take the spotlight. John's humility was a reflection of his deep love for God and his desire to see God's plan fulfilled, and this is what made him truly great in the eyes of Jesus. As we reflect on the life of John the Baptist, we can learn from his example of humility and seek to live our lives in a way that brings glory to God, rather than seeking recognition or fame for ourselves. John's greatness was not in his own power or influence, but in his humble submission to God's will and his unwavering commitment to pointing people to Jesus. This is what made John the Baptist great, and it is a lesson that we can all apply to our own lives as we seek to follow Christ and live for His glory.

Chapter 4 - Moral Courage

John the Baptist was a figure marked by incredible moral courage, and this is one of the defining aspects of what made him great according to the Bible. His willingness to speak the truth, confront sin, and stand up to powerful figures like Herod, even at the cost of his own life, shows the depth of his courage and conviction. John's fearlessness in the face of danger is emphasized, especially when he boldly confronted King Herod for his immoral actions. Herod, who was the ruler at the time, had taken his brother Philip's wife, Herodias, as his own, which was clearly against God's law. John the Baptist didn't shy away from speaking out against this sin, even though he knew it would put him in a dangerous position. He told Herod directly, "It is not lawful for thee to have thy brother's wife" (Mark 6:18). This fearless confrontation is a key example of John's moral courage. Most people would have been afraid to challenge someone as powerful as Herod, but John didn't let fear stop him from standing up for what was right. He was fully aware that speaking out against a ruler's sin could lead to imprisonment or worse, but his commitment to God's truth was stronger than his fear of the consequences. John's courage wasn't just about his willingness to confront Herod; it was also about his unwavering dedication to proclaiming God's message, no matter the cost. He wasn't afraid to call out sin wherever he saw it, whether it was among the religious leaders of the day, the common people, or the ruling authorities. John's moral courage set him apart from many others because he didn't compromise his message to avoid conflict or gain favor with those in power. He was bold and fearless, trusting that God's truth was more important than his own safety or reputation. John the Baptist's moral courage also extended to his message of repentance, which he preached to all who would listen. He called people to turn away from their sins and prepare their hearts for the coming of the Messiah. His message wasn't always easy to hear, and it certainly wasn't popular with everyone, but John was faithful in delivering it. He didn't water down his message to make it more palatable or to avoid offending people. Instead, he preached the truth with conviction, knowing that true repentance required confronting sin head-on. This boldness in preaching repentance is another aspect of John's moral courage. He wasn't concerned with being liked or accepted by the people around him. His only concern was fulfilling the mission that God had given him, which was to prepare the way for Jesus Christ by calling people to repentance. John's courage in preaching this message, even when it made people uncomfortable or angry, is part of what made him such a powerful figure in the Bible. Even though John's message was difficult for many to hear, it was necessary. The people of Israel needed to be reminded of their need for repentance and to turn back to God. John's courage in delivering this message shows his deep love for God and for the people he was called to serve. He didn't shy away from telling the truth, even when it was hard, because he knew that true repentance was the only way for people to be ready for the coming of the Messiah. John's moral courage is perhaps most vividly displayed in his interactions with Herod and Herodias. After John confronted Herod about his unlawful marriage to Herodias, Herodias became furious. She held a grudge against John and wanted to have him killed, but Herod was afraid to execute him because he knew that John was a righteous and holy man (Mark 6:19-20). However, Herodias eventually found a way to get what she wanted. During Herod's birthday celebration, her daughter, Salome, danced for Herod and his guests, and Herod was so pleased that he promised to give her whatever she asked for, up to half of his kingdom. Prompted by her mother, Salome asked for the head of John the Baptist on a platter. Herod, though distressed by this request, felt trapped by his own promise and the pressure of his guests, so he ordered John to be executed (Mark 6:21-28). John's death was the ultimate consequence of his moral courage. He had spoken out against Herod's sin, knowing full well that it could cost him his life, and in the end, it did. However, even in the face of death, John never wavered in his commitment to God's truth. His courage remained strong until the very end, and his willingness to sacrifice his life rather than compromise on his convictions is a testament to his greatness. John's moral courage wasn't just about standing up to Herod; it was about his entire approach to life and ministry. From the very beginning of his ministry, John demonstrated a fearless commitment to doing what was right in God's eyes, no matter the personal cost. He lived a life of simplicity and humility, choosing to dwell in the wilderness and wear rough clothing made of camel's hair, rather than seeking the comforts or recognition of the world (Matthew 3:4). This lifestyle reflected his deep conviction that his purpose in life was to serve God and prepare the way for Jesus, not to seek his own glory or comfort. John's courage was also evident in how he confronted the religious leaders of his time, the Pharisees and Sadducees, who were often more concerned with outward appearances and strict adherence to religious rules than with true repentance and a heart that sought after God. When they came to observe his baptisms, John boldly rebuked them, calling them a "generation of vipers" and warning them of the coming judgment if they did not repent (Matthew 3:7-10). This confrontation shows that John's courage wasn't limited to challenging political rulers like Herod; he was also willing to confront religious leaders when they were leading people astray. He didn't allow the fear of opposition or the potential backlash from powerful groups to silence him. Instead, he spoke the truth boldly and without compromise, knowing that his ultimate accountability was to God, not to human authorities or institutions. Another key aspect of John's moral courage was his complete trust in God's plan. He knew that his role was to prepare the way for Jesus, and he fully embraced that role, even when it meant stepping aside as Jesus' ministry grew. John's disciples were concerned when they saw people beginning to follow Jesus instead of John, but John wasn't worried. He understood that his purpose was to point people to Jesus, not to gather followers for himself. In John 3:30, he famously said, "He must increase, but I must decrease," showing his humility and willingness to let go of his own prominence for the sake of God's plan. This attitude also required moral courage, as John had to be willing to step back and allow Jesus to take center stage, even though he had been the one preparing the way. John's courage in recognizing and accepting his role in God's plan, even when it meant decreasing in influence, is a powerful example of his greatness. John the Baptist's moral courage also serves as an example for us today. In a world where it is often easier to remain silent in the face of wrongdoing or to go along with the crowd, John's fearless stand for truth challenges us to be bold in standing up for what is right. His life reminds us that true greatness comes not from seeking our own comfort or popularity, but from being willing to speak the truth and stand up for what is right, even when it is difficult or dangerous. John's courage also reminds us that following God's will often requires sacrifice. For John, the cost of standing up for God's truth was his own life, but he was willing to pay that price because he understood that his mission was about something far greater than himself. He knew that his role in God's plan was to prepare the way for Jesus, and he was faithful to that mission until the very end, no matter the personal cost. John's moral courage is a testament to his deep faith in God and his unwavering commitment to fulfilling the purpose God had given him. In conclusion, John the Baptist's moral courage is one of the key factors that made him great. His fearless confrontation of Herod and his willingness to call out sin, even at the cost of his life, demonstrate the depth of his courage and conviction. John's boldness in preaching repentance, his unwavering commitment to God's truth, and his willingness to sacrifice his own life for the sake of righteousness all point to the greatness of his character. John's moral courage was not just about standing up to powerful figures like Herod; it was about his entire approach to life and ministry. From his humble lifestyle in the wilderness to his fearless rebuke of the Pharisees and Sadducees, John demonstrated a commitment to truth and righteousness that set him apart from others. His courage was rooted in his deep faith in God and his understanding of his role in God's plan. Even when faced with imprisonment and death, John never wavered in his commitment to proclaiming God's message. His courage serves as a powerful example for us today, reminding us that true greatness comes from standing up for what is right, even when it is difficult or dangerous. John the Baptist's life and legacy continue to inspire us to live with the same moral courage, boldness, and faithfulness that he displayed in his ministry.

Chapter 5 - Master of Simplicity

John the Baptist is a towering figure in the Bible, not because he sought power, fame, or luxury, but because he chose to live a life of simplicity, humility, and devotion to God. One of the key aspects of what made John great was his mastery of simplicity. John's life in the wilderness was a testament to his dedication to God above all else. His entire lifestyle was marked by simplicity, and it was this simplicity that allowed him to focus on his mission and remain steadfast in his commitment to prepare the way for the Messiah. While many people in the world seek comfort, wealth, and recognition, John chose a different path. He lived in the wilderness, far from the comforts and distractions of city life. His clothing was made of camel's hair, and he ate locusts and wild honey (Matthew 3:4). This simple, rugged lifestyle set John apart from the religious leaders of his time, who often lived in luxury and enjoyed the respect and privileges that came with their positions. John's choice to live simply was not just a reflection of his personal preferences—it was a deliberate decision to align his life with the mission God had given him. By rejecting worldly comforts, John was able to remain focused on his calling without being distracted by the things that often pull people away from their relationship with God. His lifestyle reflected a deep trust in God's provision and a clear understanding that true fulfillment comes not from material possessions but from living in obedience to God's will. John's simplicity was not just seen in his clothing and diet, but also in his message. He preached a straightforward message of repentance, calling people to turn away from their sins and prepare their hearts for the coming of the Kingdom of Heaven. There was nothing flashy or complicated about John's ministry—he didn't use elaborate speeches or seek to impress people with his knowledge or eloquence. Instead, he spoke with conviction and authority, delivering a message that was both powerful and simple: "Repent ye: for the kingdom of heaven is at hand" (Matthew 3:2). John's ability to deliver such a clear and compelling message was directly tied to his simple lifestyle. By choosing to live in the wilderness and distance himself from the distractions and temptations of the world, John was able to hear God's voice more clearly and remain focused on the mission he had been given. His simplicity gave him the freedom to focus on the most important thing—calling people to repentance and preparing the way for Jesus. This focus and clarity of purpose are part of what made John great. John's simple lifestyle also demonstrated his complete dependence on God. In a world where many people strive for self-sufficiency and rely on their own abilities or resources, John's life was a powerful reminder that true strength and provision come from God alone. By living in the wilderness, wearing simple clothing, and eating the most basic food, John showed that he was not reliant on the things of this world. Instead, he trusted that God would provide for his needs, and he lived a life that was fully surrendered to God's will. This level of dependence on God is another aspect of John's greatness. While many people are tempted to seek security in material possessions, John knew that his true security came from his relationship with God. He didn't need the comforts of the world because he had something far greater—a deep and abiding trust in God's faithfulness. This trust allowed him to live simply and with complete confidence in God's provision, even when his circumstances were difficult. John's simple lifestyle also reflected his humility. Unlike many of the religious leaders of his time, who sought recognition and status, John didn't seek to elevate himself or draw attention to his own greatness. In fact, he consistently pointed people away from himself and toward Jesus. When people asked him if he was the Messiah, John made it clear that he was not. He said, "I indeed baptize you with water unto repentance: but he that cometh after me is mightier than I, whose shoes I am not worthy to bear" (Matthew 3:11). John understood that his role was to prepare the way for Jesus, not to seek glory for himself. His humility was directly tied to his simple lifestyle, as he had no desire for the trappings of power or wealth. He was content to live simply and focus on his mission, knowing that his greatness came not from his own achievements but from his obedience to God. Another way that John's simplicity made him great was that it allowed him to connect with people on a deeper level. In his day, many of the religious leaders were disconnected from the common people. They lived in luxury and held positions of authority, which often created a barrier between them and the people they were supposed to serve. John, on the other hand, lived among the people in the wilderness. His simple lifestyle made him approachable, and people from all walks of life came to hear him preach. They were drawn to his authenticity and his unwavering commitment to the truth. John's simplicity allowed him to be fully present with the people he was ministering to, and this made his message even more powerful. The crowds who came to John recognized that he was different from the other religious leaders of the time. His simple lifestyle and straightforward message resonated with them because it reflected a deep sincerity and a genuine desire to see people come to repentance and be reconciled to God. John's greatness was not in his ability to impress people with his knowledge or wealth, but in his ability to lead people to God through his humility and simplicity. John's mastery of simplicity also allowed him to remain steadfast in the face of opposition. Living a simple life in the wilderness gave John the strength to stand firm in his convictions, even when he faced criticism or danger. He was not swayed by the opinions of others or by the pressures of society because his focus was solely on fulfilling the mission God had given him. This single-minded dedication to his calling is another reason why John was so great. He didn't let the distractions of the world pull him away from his purpose, and he wasn't afraid to stand up for the truth, even when it put him at odds with powerful people like King Herod. John's simplicity gave him the clarity and courage he needed to confront Herod about his sinful behavior, even though it ultimately led to his imprisonment and death (Mark 6:17-29). John's willingness to live simply and forgo worldly comforts also set a powerful example for others. His life showed that true greatness is not found in material possessions or status, but in a life fully surrendered to God's will. John's simple lifestyle challenged the people of his day—and challenges us today—to reconsider what is truly important in life. He showed that living for God and fulfilling His purposes is far more valuable than accumulating wealth or seeking the approval of others. John's mastery of simplicity is a reminder that the things of this world are temporary, but the things of God are eternal. By choosing to live simply, John was able to focus on what truly mattered—preparing the way for Jesus and calling people to repentance. His life stands as a powerful testimony to the value of simplicity and the importance of living with a clear focus on God's purposes. In a world that often values material wealth and success, John's life is a reminder that true greatness comes from a heart fully devoted to God and a life lived in obedience to His will. John the Baptist's simple lifestyle in the wilderness exemplified his dedication to God above worldly comforts. He chose to live a life that was free from the distractions and temptations of the world so that he could focus entirely on his mission to prepare the way for the Messiah. His simple clothing, diet, and way of life reflected a deep trust in God's provision and a complete surrender to God's will. John's simplicity also allowed him to deliver a clear and powerful message of repentance, unencumbered by the complexities and distractions of the world. His humility and single-minded dedication to his calling made him great in the eyes of God, and his life serves as a powerful example of what it means to live simply and fully for God's purposes. John's greatness was not found in his wealth, status, or power, but in his complete reliance on God and his unwavering commitment to fulfilling the mission God had given him. In today's world, where many people are tempted to seek fulfillment in material possessions and worldly success, John the Baptist's life is a reminder that true greatness comes from living a life of simplicity, humility, and devotion to God. His mastery of simplicity allowed him to focus on what truly mattered and to remain steadfast in his mission, even in the face of opposition and danger. John's life challenges us to consider what we are living for and whether we are truly devoted to God's purposes or distracted by the things of this world. John the Baptist was a master of simplicity, and this simplicity was a key part of what made him great. By living a life that was focused entirely on God and free from the distractions of the world, John was able to fulfill his mission with clarity, courage, and humility. His life is a powerful example of the greatness that comes from living simply and fully for God's purposes, and it continues to inspire us to pursue a life of devotion, humility, and trust in God's provision.

Chapter 6 - Mighty in Spirit

John the Baptist was undeniably one of the most significant figures in the Bible, and one of the reasons for his greatness was that he was mighty in spirit. From the very beginning, John's life was marked by a special calling and an extraordinary strength of spirit. John was filled with the Holy Ghost from his mother's womb, and this spiritual strength guided him throughout his entire life and ministry. This divine filling was a key aspect of what made John so great—he was not only called by God for a unique mission but was also empowered by the Holy Spirit to carry out that mission with boldness, conviction, and unwavering faith. The fact that John was filled with the Holy Ghost from birth is a rare and remarkable distinction. In Luke 1:15, it says, "For he shall be great in the sight of the Lord, and shall drink neither wine nor strong drink; and he shall be filled with the Holy Ghost, even from his mother's womb." This verse reveals the divine favor on John's life before he was even born. God had set him apart for a special purpose, and the Holy Spirit's presence in his life from the very beginning gave him the strength and spiritual power he would need to fulfill his calling. John's mighty spiritual strength was evident in everything he did, from his early life in the wilderness to his powerful preaching of repentance and his fearless confrontation of sin, even in the face of great personal danger. John's spiritual strength allowed him to live a life completely devoted to God and to the mission he was given. His time in the wilderness, living simply and away from the distractions of the world, was a time of spiritual preparation, where he grew even stronger in his connection with God. This separation from the world enabled him to listen to God's voice more clearly and prepared him to begin his public ministry with an intensity and authority that few could match. When John finally began his public ministry, it was clear that he was operating with a power that came from the Holy Spirit. His message of repentance was not just words—it was delivered with an authority that pierced the hearts of those who heard it. John's spiritual strength allowed him to speak with boldness and conviction, even when his message was unpopular or difficult for people to hear. He was not afraid to confront the religious leaders of his day, the Pharisees and Sadducees, calling them out for their hypocrisy and warning them that their outward displays of righteousness were meaningless if their hearts were not right with God. In Matthew 3:7-8, John says to them, "O generation of vipers, who hath warned you to flee from the wrath to come? Bring forth therefore fruits meet for repentance." This boldness in confronting those in positions of religious authority was a direct result of John's mighty spiritual strength. He was not afraid of the consequences of speaking the truth because he was filled with the Holy Spirit and knew that his ultimate allegiance was to God, not to the approval or acceptance of people. John's spiritual strength also enabled him to endure the hardships that came with his mission. Living in the wilderness, wearing simple clothes made of camel's hair, and eating locusts and wild honey (Matthew 3:4) was not an easy or comfortable lifestyle, but John embraced it because he knew that his calling was far more important than his personal comfort. His spiritual strength allowed him to resist the temptations of the world and remain focused on the mission God had given him. This dedication and strength of spirit are part of what made John so great—he was completely committed to God's will and was not swayed by the things that often distract or tempt others. Another way John's spiritual strength was evident was in his unwavering commitment to preaching repentance. His message was clear and direct: "Repent ye: for the kingdom of heaven is at hand" (Matthew 3:2). John's call to repentance was not a gentle suggestion; it was a powerful, urgent message that carried the weight of divine authority. He was not concerned with whether people liked what he had to say—he was only concerned with delivering the message that God had given him. This boldness in preaching repentance, even when it meant facing opposition or rejection, was a reflection of John's spiritual strength. He was filled with the Holy Spirit, and this gave him the courage and power to speak the truth, no matter the cost. John's spiritual strength also manifested in his humility, which is another key aspect of what made him great. Despite the large crowds that came to hear him preach and the respect he commanded from many, John never sought to elevate himself. He knew that his role was to prepare the way for Jesus, the Messiah, and he made it clear that Jesus was far greater than he was. In John 1:27, John says of Jesus, "He it is, who coming after me is preferred before me, whose shoe's latchet I am not worthy to unloose." This statement of humility reflects the strength of John's spirit because it takes great spiritual maturity and strength to remain humble in the face of admiration and respect. John's ability to keep his focus on Jesus and to continually point people toward the Messiah, rather than seeking glory for himself, was a result of the Holy Spirit's work in his life. His spiritual strength allowed him to fulfill his mission with integrity and humility, always keeping God's glory at the forefront of everything he did. One of the most powerful examples of John's spiritual strength is seen in his interactions with Jesus. When Jesus came to John to be baptized, John initially resisted, saying, "I have need to be baptized of thee, and comest thou to me?" (Matthew 3:14). John recognized Jesus' greatness and felt unworthy to baptize Him, but when Jesus insisted, John humbly obeyed. This moment of obedience, even when John didn't fully understand why Jesus needed to be baptized, reflects his deep trust in God's plan and his willingness to follow the leading of the Holy Spirit. After baptizing Jesus, John witnessed an incredible confirmation of Jesus' identity as the Messiah. In Matthew 3:16-17, it says, "And Jesus, when he was baptized, went up straightway out of the water: and, lo, the heavens were opened unto him, and he saw the Spirit of God descending like a dove, and lighting upon him: And lo a voice from heaven, saying, This is my beloved Son, in whom I am well pleased." John's spiritual strength allowed him to play a crucial role in this moment, which marked the beginning of Jesus' public ministry. John's willingness to obey, even when it didn't make sense to him at the time, is a testament to the strength of his spirit and his deep connection with God. John's spiritual strength was also evident in his ability to endure hardship and persecution. After boldly confronting King Herod for his unlawful marriage to his brother's wife, Herodias, John was arrested and imprisoned (Mark 6:17-18). This was a difficult and dangerous situation, but even in prison, John's spirit remained strong. He didn't lose faith in God or question his mission, though he did experience a moment of doubt, which only highlights the human side of John's story. In Matthew 11:2-3, while John was in prison, he sent his disciples to ask Jesus, "Art thou he that should come, or do we look for another?" This moment of doubt shows that even someone as mighty in spirit as John had times when he needed reassurance, but it also shows the strength of his spirit in that he sought answers from Jesus directly, rather than turning away in despair. Jesus' response to John's disciples was not one of rebuke but of confirmation and encouragement. Jesus said, "Go and shew John again those things which ye do hear and see: The blind receive their sight, and the lame walk, the lepers are cleansed, and the deaf hear, the dead are raised up, and the poor have the gospel preached to them. And blessed is he, whosoever shall not be offended in me" (Matthew 11:4-6). Jesus acknowledged John's greatness in the very next verses, saying, "Among them that are born of women there hath not risen a greater than John the Baptist" (Matthew 11:11). This statement from Jesus is one of the highest commendations anyone could receive and further emphasizes John's greatness, rooted in his mighty spiritual strength. Even in moments of doubt, John's spirit remained strong, and his faith in God was ultimately reaffirmed. John's spiritual strength was also evident in his willingness to sacrifice everything for the sake of his mission. His boldness in speaking the truth, even when it meant confronting powerful leaders like Herod, ultimately led to his death. Herodias, angry with John for exposing her sin, manipulated her daughter, Salome, into asking for John's head on a platter during a feast (Mark 6:21-29). Herod, though reluctant, complied with the request, and John was executed. John's death was a result of his unwavering commitment to preaching God's truth and his refusal to compromise, even in the face of death. His spiritual strength gave him the courage to remain faithful to his calling, no matter the cost, and this ultimate sacrifice further highlights the greatness of his character. John the Baptist's life was marked by spiritual strength in every aspect. From the moment he was filled with the Holy Ghost in his mother's womb to his bold preaching of repentance, his humility in the face of admiration, his obedience to God's will, and his courage in the face of persecution, John demonstrated a mighty spirit that was empowered by God. His strength of spirit allowed him to fulfill his mission with integrity, humility, and unwavering faithfulness, even unto death. John's life serves as a powerful example of what it means to be mighty in spirit, and his legacy continues to inspire us to seek the strength that comes from being filled with the Holy Spirit and living in obedience to God's will. John the Baptist's greatness was not rooted in worldly power, wealth, or status, but in his spiritual strength and his complete dependence on God. His life reminds us that true greatness comes from being filled with the Holy Spirit and living a life fully devoted to God's purposes, no matter the cost. John's mighty spirit made him one of the greatest figures in the Bible, and his example challenges us to pursue that same strength of spirit in our own lives, trusting in God's power and provision every step of the way.

Chapter 7 - Model of Faithfulness

John the Baptist stands out in the Bible as a model of faithfulness, and this unwavering commitment to his calling is one of the key reasons he is considered great. From the moment his life was foretold, to his powerful ministry in the wilderness, and even through his imprisonment and eventual death, John remained steadfast and devoted to the purpose God had set for him. His story is one of dedication, perseverance, and courage, making him an inspiring figure whose faithfulness in the face of doubt and hardship is something we can all learn from. One of the most striking aspects of John's faithfulness is how it began before he was even born. In Luke 1:15, the angel told John's father, Zechariah, that John would be "great in the sight of the Lord" and that he would be filled with the Holy Ghost from his mother's womb. This special calling set John apart from birth, and his faithfulness to that calling defined the rest of his life. Even as a child, John was growing and becoming strong in spirit, preparing for the important work God had in store for him. His faithfulness was evident from a young age, as he lived a life of simplicity and devotion, even choosing to live in the wilderness to be fully focused on God's will for his life.

John's faithfulness was also clear in his unwavering dedication to preaching repentance and preparing the way for the coming of the Messiah. In Matthew 3:1-2, it says, "In those days came John the Baptist, preaching in the wilderness of Judaea, and saying, Repent ye: for the kingdom of heaven is at hand." John didn't waver in his message, even when it meant challenging the religious leaders of his day or facing criticism from others. He boldly called people to repent and turn back to God, knowing that his role was to prepare their hearts for the coming of Jesus. John's entire ministry was built on faithfulness to this calling, and he didn't let anything distract him from the mission God had given him. His single-minded dedication to preaching the truth, even when it wasn't popular, is a powerful example of faithfulness in action. One of the ways John's faithfulness shines through is in how he handled the attention he received. Many people came to hear John preach, and his message drew large crowds. People were moved by his words and saw him as a prophet. Some even wondered if he might be the Messiah. But John, in his faithfulness, never sought to take the glory for himself. He made it clear from the beginning that he was not the Christ but was sent to prepare the way for Him. In John 1:20, it says, "And he confessed, and denied not; but confessed, I am not the Christ." John's humility and faithfulness to his mission are shown in this simple but powerful statement. He didn't seek to elevate himself, even though he had the attention and admiration of many. Instead, he continually pointed people to Jesus, knowing that his role was to direct people to the true Savior. John's faithfulness was grounded in a deep understanding of his purpose and his place in God's plan. His whole life was about preparing the way for Jesus, and he was faithful to that mission from the beginning until the end. One of the most memorable moments of John's ministry is when Jesus came to him to be baptized. At first, John was hesitant, feeling unworthy to baptize the Messiah. In Matthew 3:14, John says, "I have need to be baptized of thee, and comest thou to me?" But when Jesus insisted, John faithfully obeyed, baptizing Jesus in the Jordan River. This act of obedience, even in the face of his own feelings of inadequacy, shows John's commitment to fulfilling God's will, no matter how challenging or unexpected it might be. John's faithfulness was not about understanding everything perfectly; it was about trusting God and being obedient, even when he didn't fully comprehend why things were happening the way they were. This moment of baptism was not just a significant event in the life of Jesus, but also a profound demonstration of John's faithfulness to his calling. Even when it seemed that his role might be finished or when others might have been tempted to hold on to the spotlight, John stepped aside and allowed Jesus to take center stage. He understood that his mission was to prepare the way for the Messiah, and once Jesus had begun His public ministry, John was content to decrease so that Jesus could increase. In John 3:30, John says, "He must increase, but I must decrease." This is a powerful example of faithfulness, as John was not concerned with his own status or recognition. He was faithful to the mission God had given him, even when it meant stepping back and letting Jesus take the lead. John's faithfulness was also evident in his courage to speak the truth, no matter the consequences. One of the most striking examples of this is when John confronted King Herod about his unlawful marriage to Herodias, his brother's wife. In Mark 6:18, John said to Herod, "It is not lawful for thee to have thy brother's wife." This bold proclamation of truth ultimately led to John's imprisonment and eventual death, but John remained faithful to God's truth, even in the face of danger. He didn't compromise his message or water down the truth to avoid conflict. Instead, he stood firm in his convictions, knowing that faithfulness to God's word was more important than his own safety. This kind of faithfulness requires incredible courage, and John's willingness to stand up to powerful rulers like Herod, even when it meant risking his life, shows just how deeply committed he was to his calling.

Even when John was imprisoned for speaking the truth, he remained faithful to God. However, it's important to note that John, like all of us, had moments of doubt. While he was in prison, John sent some of his disciples to ask Jesus, "Art thou he that should come, or do we look for another?" (Matthew 11:3). This moment of doubt does not diminish John's faithfulness; in fact, it makes his faithfulness even more relatable and powerful. Despite being filled with the Holy Spirit from birth and having spent his life preparing the way for Jesus, John still had questions when he found himself in difficult circumstances. But even in his doubt, John didn't turn away from his calling or lose faith in God's plan. Instead, he sought answers from Jesus, demonstrating that true faithfulness doesn't mean never having doubts—it means continuing to seek God and trust in His plan, even when things are unclear or when we are going through difficult times. Jesus' response to John's question was a beautiful affirmation of John's faithfulness. In Matthew 11:4-6, Jesus answered, "Go and shew John again those things which ye do hear and see: The blind receive their sight, and the lame walk, the lepers are cleansed, and the deaf hear, the dead are raised up, and the poor have the gospel preached to them." Jesus reminded John of the miraculous works that were happening, affirming that He was indeed the Messiah. Then, in Matthew 11:11, Jesus gave one of the highest commendations anyone could receive, saying, "Verily I say unto you, Among them that are born of women there hath not risen a greater than John the Baptist." This statement from Jesus is a powerful testament to John's greatness and his faithfulness to his calling. Even amid doubt and imprisonment, John remained faithful to the mission God had given him, and Jesus recognized and honored that faithfulness. John's faithfulness was not just about the big moments in his life, like baptizing Jesus or confronting Herod. It was also about his daily commitment to living out the calling God had placed on his life. John's decision to live in the wilderness, to wear simple clothing made of camel's hair, and to eat locusts and wild honey (Matthew 3:4) was a reflection of his faithfulness to God's call. He chose a life of simplicity and devotion, setting aside the comforts and distractions of the world so that he could focus entirely on fulfilling his mission. This daily faithfulness is part of what made John so great—he was not just faithful in the big, public moments, but also in the quiet, personal decisions that shaped his life and ministry. John's faithfulness extended to his final moments on earth. Even when he was imprisoned and facing the threat of execution, John remained steadfast in his commitment to the truth. He didn't recant his message or try to bargain for his life. Instead, he remained faithful to the end, trusting that God's plan was greater than his own circumstances. John's eventual death at the hands of Herodias, who held a grudge against him for exposing her sin, was a tragic end to a life of faithfulness. But even in his death, John's legacy of faithfulness lives on. His unwavering commitment to his calling, even amid doubts and imprisonment, is a powerful example for all of us of what it means to be faithful to God's purpose for our lives.

In conclusion, John the Baptist was a model of faithfulness, and it was this unwavering commitment to his calling that made him great. From the moment he was born, John was set apart for a special purpose, and he remained faithful to that purpose throughout his life. Whether he was preaching repentance in the wilderness, baptizing Jesus in the Jordan River, or confronting powerful leaders like Herod, John's faithfulness to God's mission never wavered. Even in moments of doubt and imprisonment, John continued to seek God and remain faithful to the truth

he had been called to proclaim. His life serves as a powerful reminder that true faithfulness is not about never having doubts or struggles, but about continuing to trust in God and be obedient to His will, no matter the circumstances. John's faithfulness, both in the big moments and in the daily decisions of his life, is a testament to the greatness that comes from living a life fully devoted to God's purpose. His example challenges us to remain faithful to our own callings, trusting that God's plan is greater than anything we could imagine, and that faithfulness to His will is the path to true greatness.

Chapter 8 - Messenger of Judgment

John the Baptist was a powerful and influential figure in the Bible, and one of the key aspects that made him great was his role as a Messenger of Judgment. He wasn't just known for preaching about salvation and the coming of the Messiah, but also for boldly proclaiming the reality of God's coming judgment. This combination of messages — salvation and judgment — made John's ministry unique and critical in preparing the hearts of the people for the arrival of Jesus Christ. John's message is clear, direct, and at times, frightening because he wanted people to understand that while God offers salvation, there are also consequences for sin, and the judgment of God is inevitable for those who do not repent. John didn't shy away from delivering this truth, even though it was uncomfortable and not popular. His willingness to confront people with the reality of judgment is one of the reasons he is considered so great in the Bible. His boldness in declaring that judgment was coming demonstrated his commitment to God's truth and his deep concern for the spiritual condition of those he preached to.

John's message of judgment is first seen in his call for repentance. In Matthew 3:1-2, it says, "In those days came John the Baptist, preaching in the wilderness of Judaea, and saying, Repent ye: for the kingdom of heaven is at hand." This call to repentance was not just a suggestion or a nice idea; it was a warning. The kingdom of heaven was near, and people needed to repent because God's judgment was coming. John's preaching wasn't just about offering salvation to those who were ready to turn from their sins; it was also about warning those who refused to repent that they were in danger of facing God's wrath. In Matthew 3:7-8, John's message becomes even more direct when the Pharisees and Sadducees come to observe his baptisms. He says to them, "O generation of vipers, who hath warned you to flee from the wrath to come? Bring forth therefore fruits meet for repentance." In this passage, John is addressing the religious leaders, calling them out for their hypocrisy. He warns them that simply relying on their status or their heritage as descendants of Abraham won't save them from God's judgment. They needed to show true repentance through their actions, not just through empty religious rituals. John's use of the term "wrath to come" shows that he was deeply aware of the judgment that was coming and felt a strong responsibility to warn people about it. His willingness to confront even the most powerful and respected leaders of his time with the reality of God's judgment speaks to his fearlessness and his commitment to delivering the truth, no matter the cost.

John's message of judgment didn't stop with the religious leaders. He preached to everyone, from common people to soldiers and tax collectors, warning them that judgment was coming and that they needed to turn away from their sins. In Luke 3:9, John says, "And now also the axe is laid unto the root of the trees: every tree therefore which bringeth not forth good fruit is hewn down, and cast into the fire." This vivid imagery of an axe ready to cut down unfruitful trees represents the urgency of John's message. He was telling the people that God's judgment was imminent, and they didn't have much time to repent. The idea of being "cast into the fire" is a clear reference to the consequences of ignoring God's call to repentance. John didn't sugarcoat the truth. He wanted people to understand that while God is merciful and offers salvation, He is also a righteous judge who will not tolerate sin. John's message of judgment was meant to wake people up from their spiritual complacency and make them realize the seriousness of their situation.

One of the reasons John's message of judgment was so powerful was that it was rooted in his understanding of who God is. John knew that God is holy and righteous, and because of this, sin cannot go unpunished. He understood that while God offers forgiveness and salvation to those who repent, there is also a day of reckoning for those who refuse to turn from their sins. In Matthew 3:11-12, John says, "I indeed baptize you with water unto repentance. But he that cometh after me is mightier than I, whose shoes I am not worthy to bear: he shall baptize you with the Holy Ghost, and with fire: Whose fan is in his hand, and he will thoroughly purge his floor, and gather his wheat into the garner; but he will burn up the chaff with unquenchable fire." In this passage, John is speaking about Jesus, who will bring both salvation and judgment. The "wheat" represents those who have repented and are saved, while the "chaff" represents those who refuse to repent and will face God's judgment. The image of the "unquenchable fire" emphasizes the finality and seriousness of this judgment. John's role as a messenger was not just to prepare people for the coming of Jesus as Savior, but also to warn them that He would come as Judge.

John's message of judgment was not motivated by a desire to scare people or condemn them. Rather, it was motivated by love and concern for their spiritual well-being. John knew that the only way for people to avoid God's judgment was to repent and turn back to God, and he was willing to preach this difficult message because he cared deeply about their eternal destiny. His faithfulness to this message, even when it was hard to hear, is a testament to his greatness. John wasn't interested in gaining popularity or saying things that would make people feel good. He was focused on delivering the truth, even when it was uncomfortable. This is one of the reasons why so many people respected John, even if they didn't always like what he had to say. His commitment to preaching both salvation and judgment made him a powerful and effective messenger of God's truth.

Another aspect of John's greatness as a messenger of judgment is seen in his courage. Preaching about judgment is not an easy task, especially when it means confronting powerful people who don't want to hear that they are living in sin. But John was fearless in delivering his message, even when it put his life at risk. One of the most striking examples of this is when John confronted King Herod about his unlawful marriage to Herodias, his brother's wife. In Mark 6:18, John said to Herod, "It is not lawful for thee to have thy brother's wife." This bold confrontation of sin eventually led to John's imprisonment and death, but John didn't back down. He was willing to speak the truth about God's judgment, even when it meant facing persecution and danger. John's courage in the face of such opposition is a powerful example of his faithfulness to God's message. He didn't let fear of consequences stop him from delivering the truth, and this is one of the reasons he is considered so great.

Even though John's message of judgment was often difficult for people to hear, it was necessary. John understood that people needed to be confronted with the reality of their sin in order to fully appreciate the gift of salvation that Jesus was offering. Without an understanding of God's judgment, people might be tempted to take God's grace for granted or to think that they could continue living in sin without consequences. John's message of judgment served as a wake-up call, reminding people that God is holy and that sin has serious consequences. At the same time, John's message of judgment was always paired with a message of hope. He didn't just warn people about God's judgment; he also offered them a way to escape it through repentance. In Luke 3:3, it says that John "came into all the country about Jordan, preaching the baptism of repentance for the remission of sins." John's call to repentance was an invitation to turn away from sin and receive forgiveness. He made it clear that while God's judgment was real, so was His mercy. For those who were willing to repent, there was the promise of salvation and a new life in the Kingdom of Heaven.

John's message of judgment and repentance paved the way for Jesus' ministry. When Jesus began preaching, He echoed many of the same themes that John had emphasized, including the call to repentance and the warning of God's coming judgment. In Matthew 4:17, it says, "From that time Jesus began to preach, and to say, Repent: for the kingdom of heaven is at hand." Jesus, like John, understood the importance of repentance and the reality of God's judgment. John's role as a messenger of judgment was crucial in preparing people's hearts to receive Jesus' message. By warning people about the consequences of sin and the urgency of repentance, John helped them understand their need for a Savior.

In conclusion, what made John the Baptist great was not only his role as a messenger of salvation but also his role as a Messenger of Judgment. John's bold and fearless preaching about God's coming judgment set him apart as a powerful and faithful servant of God. He didn't shy away from delivering the hard truths, even when it meant confronting powerful leaders like the Pharisees, Sadducees, and King Herod. John's message of judgment was motivated by a deep concern for the spiritual well-being of the people, and he was willing to face opposition and persecution in order to deliver God's truth. His courage, faithfulness, and commitment to preaching both salvation and judgment made him a key figure in preparing the way for Jesus. John's life and ministry remind us that while God offers grace and forgiveness, there is also a reality of judgment for those who refuse to repent. John's greatness lies in his ability to hold these two truths together, offering both a warning and an invitation. He called people to repentance, knowing that God's judgment was near, but also offering them the hope of salvation if they were willing to turn from their sins and follow God. John's faithfulness to this message, even at the cost of his own life, makes him one of the greatest figures in the Bible and a powerful example of what it means to be a true messenger of God's truth.

Chapter 9 - Magnified by Jesus

John the Baptist holds a unique and remarkable place in the Bible, and one of the clearest indications of his greatness is found in Jesus' own words. In Matthew 11:11, Jesus says, "Verily I say unto you, Among them that are born of women there hath not risen a greater than John the Baptist: notwithstanding he that is least in the kingdom of heaven is greater than he". This powerful statement, made by Jesus Himself, magnifies the importance and significance of John the Baptist in God's plan for humanity. The fact that Jesus, the Son of God, would declare John as the greatest among those born of women speaks volumes about the role John played and the qualities that made him so exceptional. Jesus' declaration of John's greatness highlights the depth of John's character, his unwavering commitment to God's mission, his humility, and his role as the forerunner of Christ. By examining what Jesus meant when He magnified John's greatness, we can better understand why John the Baptist is considered such an important and influential figure in the Bible, and why his life serves as an example of dedication, faithfulness, and humility.

To truly grasp the significance of Jesus' statement about John, we must first look at the context of John's life and ministry. John the Baptist was born to Zechariah and Elizabeth, a couple who were considered righteous before God but had been childless for many years. The angel Gabriel appeared to Zechariah to announce that Elizabeth would bear a son, and this son, John, would be filled with the Holy Spirit from his mother's womb and would be the one to prepare the way for the Lord (Luke 1:13-17). John's life was marked by divine purpose even before he was born, and this sense of calling and mission shaped everything he did. From his early life in the wilderness to his bold and uncompromising preaching of repentance, John demonstrated an extraordinary commitment to the mission God had given him. John's greatness, as magnified by Jesus, was not based on worldly success, wealth, or power, but on his complete dedication to God's plan and his willingness to live a life of humility and sacrifice.

One of the key aspects of John's greatness that Jesus highlights is his role as the forerunner of the Messiah. John's entire ministry was focused on preparing the people of Israel for the coming of Jesus. He preached a message of repentance, calling people to turn away from their sins and be baptized as a sign of their commitment to following God. In Matthew 3:1-2, it says, "In those days came John the Baptist, preaching in the wilderness of Judaea, and saying, Repent ye: for the kingdom of heaven is at hand." John's message was clear and direct, and it was designed to prepare people's hearts for the arrival of Jesus. This role as the forerunner of the Messiah was a crucial part of God's plan for salvation, and John fulfilled it with incredible faithfulness and courage. Jesus magnified John's greatness because of his unique role in God's redemptive plan. No one else in history was given the responsibility of preparing the way for the Savior of the world, and John embraced this role with humility and dedication.

John's greatness is also seen in his humility, a quality that Jesus would have certainly valued and admired. Despite the large crowds that came to hear him preach and the respect he commanded from many, John never sought to elevate himself. In fact, he made it clear from the beginning that his purpose was not to draw attention to himself but to point people to Jesus. In John 1:20, when people asked if he was the Messiah, John answered, "And he confessed, and denied not; but confessed, I am not the Christ." John understood that his role was to prepare the way for someone far greater than himself, and he consistently pointed people toward Jesus. In John 3:30, John famously said, "He must increase, but I must decrease." This statement reflects the depth of John's humility and his understanding of his role in God's plan. He was content to step aside and let Jesus take center stage, knowing that his mission had always been to lead people to the Messiah, not to seek glory for himself. Jesus magnified John's greatness in part because of this incredible humility. In a world where many people seek recognition and status, John's willingness to decrease so that Jesus could increase sets him apart as a true servant of God.

Another reason Jesus magnified John's greatness is his unwavering commitment to truth and righteousness, even in the face of opposition. John was not afraid to speak out against sin, no matter who was involved. One of the most notable examples of this is when John confronted King Herod about his unlawful marriage to Herodias, his brother's wife. In Mark 6:18, John said to Herod, "It is not lawful for thee to have thy brother's wife." This bold proclamation of truth eventually led to John's imprisonment and death, but John remained faithful to God's message, even when it meant confronting powerful leaders and facing persecution. John's courage in standing up for what was right, regardless of the personal cost, is another reason Jesus recognized his greatness. John didn't compromise his message or try to avoid conflict in order to protect himself. He was fully committed to proclaiming God's truth, even when it was difficult or dangerous.

John's greatness, as magnified by Jesus, is also connected to the power of the Holy Spirit in his life. From the moment he was conceived, John was filled with the Holy Spirit, and this divine empowerment gave him the strength and boldness to carry out his mission. In Luke 1:15, the angel Gabriel tells Zechariah that John "shall be filled with the Holy Ghost, even from his mother's womb." This spiritual anointing was a key factor in John's greatness because it enabled him to live a life completely devoted to God's will. John's connection to the Holy Spirit is evident in everything he did, from his powerful preaching to his ability to remain focused on his mission in the face of adversity. Jesus magnified John's greatness in part because of this special anointing and the way John allowed the Holy Spirit to guide and empower his life and ministry.

Jesus' declaration of John's greatness also highlights the idea that true greatness in God's kingdom is not measured by worldly standards. In Matthew 11:11, Jesus says, "Among them that are born of women there hath not risen a greater than John the Baptist: notwithstanding he that is least in the kingdom of heaven is greater than he." This statement is profound because it shows that greatness in God's eyes is not about power, wealth, or status. John was great because of his faithfulness to God's calling, his humility, and his willingness to sacrifice for the sake of the gospel. However, Jesus also introduces a new way of understanding greatness in this verse. While John was the greatest among those born of women, Jesus points out that those who are part of the kingdom of heaven are even greater. This doesn't diminish John's greatness but rather highlights the incredible privilege of being part of God's kingdom through faith in Jesus Christ. John's role was to prepare the way for this new reality, where greatness is defined not by human standards but by one's relationship with God through Christ.

John's greatness is also magnified by the impact of his ministry. While his time on earth was relatively short, the legacy of his work has lasted for centuries. John's message of repentance and his role in baptizing Jesus laid the foundation for Jesus' public ministry. In Matthew 3:13-17, we read about the moment when Jesus came to John to be baptized. At first, John was hesitant, saying, "I have need to be baptized of thee, and comest thou to me?" (Matthew 3:14). But Jesus insisted, and John obediently baptized Him. This moment was a pivotal event in the life of Jesus, marking the beginning of His public ministry and the moment when the heavens opened and God declared, "This is my beloved Son, in whom I am well pleased" (Matthew 3:17). John's faithfulness in carrying out this act of obedience further highlights his greatness. His role in baptizing Jesus was not only a fulfillment of prophecy but also a confirmation of his mission as the one who would prepare the way for the Messiah.

In addition to his role as the forerunner of Christ, John's greatness is magnified by the fact that he remained faithful to his mission until the very end of his life. Even when he was imprisoned by Herod for speaking out against his sin, John didn't waver in his commitment to God's truth. In Matthew 11:2-3, we read about how John, while in prison, sent his disciples to ask Jesus, "Art thou he that should come, or do we look for another?" This question reveals that even someone as great as John had moments of doubt, especially in the face of suffering and uncertainty. However, rather than turning away from his faith, John sought reassurance from Jesus. Jesus' response to John's disciples was not one of rebuke but of affirmation. He told them to report back to John the miracles they had seen: "The blind receive their sight, and the lame walk, the lepers are cleansed, and the deaf hear, the dead are raised up, and the poor have the gospel preached to them" (Matthew 11:5). Jesus' message to John was a reminder that the kingdom of God was indeed being established, just as John had preached. Even in his moments of doubt, John remained faithful, and this perseverance in the face of hardship further magnifies his greatness.

In conclusion, what made John the Baptist great was not just his role as the forerunner of Christ but also his faithfulness, humility, courage, and dedication to God's mission. Jesus' declaration in Matthew 11:11 magnifies John's greatness by highlighting the unique and important role he played in God's plan for salvation. John's life serves as a powerful example of what it means to be truly great in God's eyes. His greatness was not based on worldly standards of success but on his complete devotion to God's will, his willingness to point others to Jesus, and his unwavering commitment to proclaiming the truth, even in the face of opposition. John the Baptist's legacy continues to inspire believers today, reminding us that true greatness comes from faithfully following God's calling, no matter the cost, and always seeking to magnify Jesus, just as John did throughout his life.

Chapter 10 - Miracle of His Birth

John the Baptist was a figure of great significance in the Bible, and one of the key aspects that made him so extraordinary was the miracle of his birth. The circumstances surrounding his birth were nothing short of miraculous, and these events signaled his divine calling and the special role he would play in preparing the way for Jesus Christ. John's birth was not an ordinary one, and the supernatural elements surrounding it highlight that God had set John apart for a unique and vital purpose. The Bible recounts the story of John's birth with great detail, showing how God's hand was involved from the very beginning of John's life. From the announcement of his birth to his elderly parents, Zechariah and Elizabeth, to the fulfillment of the angel Gabriel's words, every part of John's birth points to the fact that he was chosen by God for an extraordinary mission. His birth itself is a testament to God's power, and it set the stage for the life of greatness that John would lead as the forerunner of the Messiah. Understanding the miraculous circumstances of John's birth helps us see why he is considered one of the greatest figures in the Bible, and it underscores the divine nature of his calling.

The story of John the Baptist's birth begins with his parents, Zechariah and Elizabeth, who were both righteous before God but had no children because Elizabeth was barren. They were also well advanced in years, making it seem impossible for them to have a child. In Luke 1:6-7, it says, "And they were both righteous before God, walking in all the commandments and ordinances of the Lord blameless. And they had no child, because that Elisabeth was barren, and they both were now well stricken in years." This sets the stage for the miracle that was about to happen. Despite their faithfulness and righteousness, Zechariah and Elizabeth had given up hope of ever having a child, as they were past the age of childbearing. But God had a different plan for them, one that would not only bless them with a child but also bring about the birth of one of the greatest prophets in history. The fact that John's birth was to occur under these seemingly impossible circumstances shows that God's power was at work from the very beginning. It also signals that John's life would be marked by divine intervention and purpose.

The miracle of John's birth was first announced to Zechariah while he was serving as a priest in the temple. This was no ordinary moment—it was a time of deep spiritual significance for Zechariah, as he was offering incense in the temple, and the people were outside praying. In the midst of this sacred moment, the angel Gabriel appeared to Zechariah to deliver the news that he and Elizabeth would have a son. In Luke 1:11-13, it says, "And there appeared unto him an angel of the Lord standing on the right side of the altar of incense. And when Zechariah saw him, he was troubled, and fear fell upon him. But the angel said unto him, Fear not, Zechariah: for thy prayer is heard; and thy wife Elisabeth shall bear thee a son, and thou shalt call his name John." This angelic announcement was the first indication that John's birth would be a miraculous event. Zechariah and Elizabeth had likely prayed for a child for many years, but now, in their old age, those prayers were being answered in a way that defied all natural expectations. The appearance of the angel Gabriel also emphasizes the importance of John's birth. Angels often appeared in the Bible to deliver messages of great significance, and Gabriel's presence here signals that John's birth was part of God's divine plan for the salvation of humanity.

Gabriel's message to Zechariah didn't just announce that he and Elizabeth would have a son; it also revealed the extraordinary nature of the child who was to be born. Gabriel explained that John would have a special mission, one that was ordained by God from before his birth. In Luke 1:15-17, Gabriel says of John, "For he shall be great in the sight of the Lord, and shall drink neither wine nor strong drink; and he shall be filled with the Holy Ghost, even from his mother's womb. And many of the children of Israel shall he turn to the Lord their God. And he shall go before him in the spirit and power of Elias, to turn the hearts of the fathers to the children, and the disobedient to the wisdom of the just; to make ready a people prepared for the Lord." This description of John's future ministry shows that he was chosen by God for a specific and vital role: to prepare the people of Israel for the coming of the Messiah, Jesus Christ. The fact that John would be filled with the Holy Spirit even from his mother's womb is another indication of the miraculous nature of his life. Most people in the Bible are described as being filled with the Holy Spirit at some point in their lives, often during a moment of calling or consecration. But for John, this filling of the Spirit happened before he was even born, signaling the unique and divine nature of his mission. John was set apart by God for greatness, and his entire life would be devoted to fulfilling the purpose that God had for him.

Despite the incredible news delivered by Gabriel, Zechariah initially struggled to believe that such a miracle could happen. After all, he and Elizabeth were old, and Elizabeth had been barren her whole life. In Luke 1:18, Zechariah asked the angel, "Whereby shall I know this? for I am an old man, and my wife well stricken in years." Zechariah's doubt is understandable from a human perspective, but it also shows the natural limitations of faith when confronted with the miraculous. In response to Zechariah's doubt, Gabriel declared that because Zechariah had not believed his words, he would be unable to speak until the day the child was born. In Luke 1:20, Gabriel says, "And behold, thou shalt be dumb, and not able to speak, until the day that these things shall be performed, because thou believest not my words, which shall be fulfilled in their season." This temporary muteness served as both a sign and a consequence for Zechariah's lack of faith, but it also highlighted the certainty of God's plan. Despite Zechariah's initial doubt, the miracle of John's birth would still come to pass, just as Gabriel had said.

As time passed, Elizabeth did indeed conceive, and the miraculous nature of her pregnancy became evident to all who knew her. In Luke 1:24-25, it says, "And after those days his wife Elisabeth conceived, and hid herself five months, saying, Thus hath the Lord dealt with me in the days wherein he looked on me, to take away my reproach among men." Elizabeth's joy and gratitude are clear in this passage. In the ancient world, being childless was often seen as a source of shame or reproach, and Elizabeth's barrenness had likely been a source of great sorrow for her. But now, through this miraculous pregnancy, God had taken away her reproach and blessed her with a child who would go on to do great things for the kingdom of God. The fact that Elizabeth conceived in her old age, after a lifetime of barrenness, is a powerful reminder of God's ability to do the impossible. This miracle of conception was not just a blessing for Zechariah and Elizabeth; it was a sign that God's plan for salvation was unfolding, and that John the Baptist would play a key role in that plan.

As Elizabeth's pregnancy progressed, another miraculous event occurred that further confirmed the divine nature of John's birth. Elizabeth's relative, Mary, who had also experienced a miraculous conception, came to visit her. Mary was pregnant with Jesus, the Son of God, and when she entered Elizabeth's home, something incredible happened. In Luke 1:41-44, it says, "And it came to pass, that, when Elisabeth heard the salutation of Mary, the babe leaped in her womb; and Elisabeth was filled with the Holy Ghost: And she spake out with a loud voice, and said, Blessed art thou among women, and blessed is the fruit of thy womb. And whence is this to me, that the mother of my Lord should come to me? For, lo, as soon as the voice of thy salutation sounded in mine ears, the babe leaped in my womb for joy." This passage reveals that even before he was born, John recognized the presence of the Messiah. The fact that John leaped for joy in his mother's womb when Mary, carrying Jesus, entered the room is another sign of his divine calling. John's life was connected to the life of Jesus from the very beginning, and even in the womb, John was filled with the Holy Spirit and rejoiced in the presence of the Savior.

When the time came for John to be born, the miraculous nature of his birth continued to unfold. Elizabeth gave birth to a healthy son, and when it was time to name the child, the people assumed that he would be named after his father, Zechariah. But Elizabeth, following the instructions given by Gabriel, insisted that his name would be John. In Luke 1:60-61, it says, "And his mother answered and said, Not so; but he shall be called John. And they said unto her, There is none of thy kindred that is called by this name." The people were confused by this unusual choice of name, as it was customary to name a child after a family member. But when they asked Zechariah, who was still unable to speak, he confirmed the name by writing it on a tablet. In Luke 1:63-64, it says, "And he asked for a writing table, and wrote, saying, His name is John. And they marveled all. And his mouth was opened immediately, and his tongue loosed, and he spake, and praised God." The moment Zechariah confirmed the name John, his speech was miraculously restored, and he immediately began to praise God. This miraculous event further confirmed that John's birth was part of God's divine plan, and it caused everyone who witnessed it to marvel at what had taken place.

After his speech was restored, Zechariah, filled with the Holy Spirit, prophesied about his son's future and the role he would play in God's plan of salvation. In Luke 1:76-79, Zechariah says of John, "And thou, child, shalt be called the prophet of the Highest: for thou shalt go before the face of the Lord to prepare his ways; To give knowledge of salvation unto his people by the remission of their sins, Through the tender mercy of our God; whereby the dayspring from on high hath visited us, To give light to them that sit in darkness and in the shadow of death, to guide our feet into the way of peace." This prophecy confirms that John's life was divinely appointed, and that his mission would be to prepare the way for Jesus, the Messiah. John would be the one to announce the coming of the Savior and call people to repentance, making their hearts ready to receive the message of salvation.

In conclusion, the miracle of John the Baptist's birth is a key aspect of what made him great. From the angelic announcement to his elderly parents, to the supernatural events surrounding his conception and birth, every part of John's life was marked by God's divine intervention. His birth was a clear sign that God had chosen him for a special purpose, and the miraculous circumstances of his birth set the stage for the extraordinary life he would lead as the forerunner of Jesus Christ. John's birth was a testament to God's power and faithfulness, and it signaled the beginning of a new chapter in God's plan for salvation. John's greatness, as magnified by Jesus, was rooted in the fact that he was divinely appointed from the very beginning to prepare the way for the Messiah. The miracle of his birth reminds us that God is able to do the impossible and that He often works through unexpected and miraculous circumstances to accomplish His purposes. John the Baptist's life serves as a powerful example of what it means to be called by God and to faithfully fulfill that calling, no matter the challenges or obstacles that may arise. His story continues to inspire believers today, reminding us of the miraculous ways in which God works in our lives and the importance of responding to His call with faith and obedience.

Chapter 11 - Misunderstood but Steadfast

John the Baptist was one of the most remarkable figures in the Bible, and what made him truly great was his unwavering commitment to his mission, even in the face of being misunderstood by both his followers and his critics. Throughout his life and ministry, John encountered many people who either misinterpreted his message, questioned his methods, or outright opposed him, yet he never wavered in his dedication to preparing the way for the Messiah. John is portrayed as a man of immense faith, courage, and determination, who remained steadfast despite the misunderstandings and opposition he faced. This aspect of John's life is a testament to his greatness, as it shows how deeply rooted he was in his calling and how willing he was to endure criticism and rejection for the sake of fulfilling God's plan. Being misunderstood can be one of the most challenging experiences for anyone, yet John handled it with grace, humility, and a steadfast commitment to the truth. His ability to stay true to his mission, even when those around him didn't fully understand or appreciate what he was doing, highlights his spiritual strength and his unwavering faith in God's purpose for his life.

One of the most significant ways in which John was misunderstood was in the expectations that people had about his role and identity. Many of the people who came to hear John preach were deeply moved by his message of repentance and his bold proclamation of the coming Kingdom of God. However, some of these followers began to wonder if John might be more than just a prophet. They wondered if perhaps he was the Messiah himself. In Luke 3:15, it says, "And as the people were in expectation, and all men mused in their hearts of John, whether he were the Christ, or not." This misunderstanding about John's identity was a clear example of how people didn't fully grasp the role that John was playing. They saw his power and authority, and they were so impressed by his message that they began to think he might be the long-awaited Savior. But John, in his humility and steadfastness, was quick to correct them. In Luke 3:16, he responded, saying, "I indeed baptize you with water; but one mightier than I cometh, the latchet of whose shoes I am not worthy to unloose: he shall baptize you with the Holy Ghost and with fire." John made it clear that he was not the Christ but was merely the one sent to prepare the way for Him. Despite being misunderstood by his followers, John didn't allow their confusion to derail him from his mission. He remained focused on pointing people to Jesus and preparing their hearts for the coming of the true Messiah. This steadfastness in the face of misunderstanding is a key part of what made John great. He didn't let the praise or expectations of others distract him from his purpose. Instead, he stayed true to the message God had given him and continued to proclaim the truth, even when people didn't fully understand.

In addition to being misunderstood by his followers, John also faced criticism and opposition from the religious leaders of his time. The Pharisees and Sadducees, who were the religious elite, saw John's ministry as a threat to their authority and were often critical of his methods and message. In Matthew 3:7, we see how John boldly addressed the Pharisees and Sadducees when they came to observe his baptisms: "But when he saw many of the Pharisees and Sadducees come to his baptism, he said unto them, O generation of vipers, who hath warned you to flee from the wrath to come?" John's sharp rebuke of these religious leaders shows that he was not afraid to call out their hypocrisy and challenge their false sense of righteousness. The Pharisees and Sadducees were often more concerned with outward appearances and strict adherence to religious laws than with true repentance and a relationship with God. John's message of repentance threatened their way of life, and as a result, they misunderstood him and rejected his message. However, John did not allow their opposition to deter him from fulfilling his mission. He continued to preach the truth with boldness and conviction, knowing that his ultimate accountability was to God, not to the religious establishment. John's ability to remain steadfast in the face of criticism and rejection from those in positions of power further highlights his greatness. He wasn't concerned with gaining the approval of men; he was focused on doing the will of God, even when it meant being misunderstood and opposed by the religious authorities.

John's experience of being misunderstood extended even to his relationship with Jesus. While John had always been clear about his role as the forerunner of the Messiah, there came a time when he faced his own doubts and questions.

While imprisoned by King Herod for speaking out against Herod's unlawful marriage, John began to wonder if Jesus was truly the Messiah he had been proclaiming. In Matthew 11:2-3, it says, "Now when John had heard in the prison the works of Christ, he sent two of his disciples, and said unto him, Art thou he that should come, or do we look for another?" This moment of doubt is particularly striking because it shows that even someone as great as John the Baptist experienced uncertainty and misunderstanding at times. John had been so steadfast in his message about Jesus, but now, in the face of imprisonment and hardship, he began to wonder if everything he had believed and preached was true. However, what's important to note is that even in his doubt, John didn't turn away from Jesus. Instead, he sought clarification and reassurance directly from the source. This willingness to seek understanding, even when he was struggling, shows John's faithfulness and his desire to remain aligned with God's will. Jesus' response to John's disciples was one of reassurance and affirmation. In Matthew 11:4-5, Jesus said, "Go and shew John again those things which ye do hear and see: The blind receive their sight, and the lame walk, the lepers are cleansed, and the deaf hear, the dead are raised up, and the poor have the gospel preached to them." Jesus pointed to the miracles He was performing as evidence that He was indeed the Messiah. This response would have brought comfort to John, even in his time of doubt, and would have reaffirmed his mission.

Despite being misunderstood by others and even experiencing moments of doubt himself, John remained steadfast in his mission until the very end. His life was marked by a deep sense of purpose, and he never wavered in his commitment to fulfilling the role God had given him. Even in prison, facing the threat of death, John continued to speak the truth and stand up for righteousness. His imprisonment by Herod came as a result of his bold confrontation of the king's sin. In Mark 6:18, it says, "For John had said unto Herod, It is not lawful for thee to have thy brother's wife." This confrontation of Herod's unlawful marriage to Herodias led to John's imprisonment and eventually to his execution. Herodias, who held a grudge against John for exposing her sin, manipulated her daughter, Salome, into asking for John's head on a platter. Herod, though reluctant, ultimately gave in to this request, and John was beheaded (Mark 6:27-28). Even in the face of death, John remained faithful to his calling. He didn't compromise his message to save himself or avoid conflict. He was willing to lay down his life for the truth, and this unwavering commitment to his mission is a testament to his greatness.

What made John the Baptist truly great was not just his role as the forerunner of Christ but also his ability to remain steadfast in the face of misunderstanding, criticism, and opposition. He didn't let the opinions of others, whether they were his followers or his critics, distract him from the mission God had given him. John knew who he was and what his purpose was, and he stayed true to that purpose even when it was difficult or when others didn't fully understand. His humility and faithfulness in pointing people to Jesus, rather than seeking glory for himself, further highlight his greatness. John could have easily allowed the admiration of his followers to inflate his ego, but instead, he consistently pointed them to Jesus, saying, "He must increase, but I must decrease" (John 3:30). This humility, combined with his steadfastness in the face of opposition, sets John apart as one of the most faithful servants of God in the Bible.

In addition to his humility and faithfulness, John's greatness is also seen in his willingness to confront sin, no matter the cost. He was not afraid to speak the truth, even when it meant confronting powerful leaders like Herod or challenging the religious authorities of his day. John's boldness in standing up for what was right, even when it led to his imprisonment and death, is a powerful example of his unwavering commitment to God's truth. He didn't seek to avoid conflict or soften his message to gain favor with others. Instead, he remained faithful to the message of repentance and the coming Kingdom of God, knowing that his ultimate accountability was to God, not to men.

John's experience of being misunderstood but remaining steadfast in his mission is something that many people can relate to, even today. We all face moments in life when others don't fully understand our motives, our actions, or our faith. Like John, we may be criticized, questioned, or even rejected by those around us. But John's example shows us the importance of staying true to the calling God has placed on our lives, even when it's difficult or when others don't understand. John's faithfulness in the face of misunderstanding reminds us that our value and purpose come from God, not from the approval or opinions of others. His life is a powerful reminder that greatness in God's kingdom is not about being understood or admired by the world but about being faithful to the mission God has given us, no matter the challenges we face.

In conclusion, what made John the Baptist great was his steadfastness in the face of misunderstanding. Throughout his life and ministry, John encountered people who didn't fully understand his message, questioned his identity, or rejected his teachings. Yet he remained firm in his mission to prepare the way for the Messiah. John's humility, courage, and unwavering faith in God's plan allowed him to continue pointing people to Jesus, even when he was misunderstood by his followers and criticized by the religious leaders. His willingness to stand up for truth and righteousness, even when it led to his imprisonment and death, further highlights his greatness. John's life is a testament to the power of faithfulness and perseverance, and it serves as an example for all of us to remain steadfast in our own callings, even when we face opposition or misunderstanding. John the Baptist's greatness was not defined by the approval of others but by his unwavering commitment to God's mission, and this is what makes him one of the most remarkable figures in the Bible.

Chapter 12 - Martyr for Righteousness

John the Baptist is one of the most extraordinary figures in the Bible, and one of the central reasons for his greatness was his unwavering commitment to righteousness, which ultimately led to him becoming a martyr for righteousness. John's life and ministry were marked by boldness, courage, and a deep sense of moral conviction. He lived according to the principles of truth, justice, and holiness, and he was not afraid to speak out against sin, no matter the cost. His willingness to stand firm in his convictions, even when it placed him in direct opposition to powerful and influential figures, showed the depth of his faith and the strength of his character. The ultimate expression of John's greatness came when he sacrificed his life for the sake of righteousness, becoming a martyr who stood unwavering in his commitment to God's truth. This selfless act of giving up his life for the truth is what sets John apart as one of the greatest figures in the Kingdom of God, as declared by Jesus Himself. His martyrdom is not just a testimony to his bravery but also a profound example of what it means to be fully dedicated to God, even unto death.

To understand the full significance of John the Baptist's martyrdom, we must first look at the events that led to his death and how they illustrate his unyielding dedication to righteousness. John's boldness in calling out sin was a hallmark of his ministry. He wasn't content to simply preach a message of repentance to the common people; he also confronted the powerful and the elite when they strayed from God's commands. One of the most notable examples of this is when John openly rebuked King Herod for his sinful actions. Herod had unlawfully married Herodias, the wife of his brother Philip, which was a direct violation of God's law. In Mark 6:18, it says, "For John had said unto Herod, It is not lawful for thee to have thy brother's wife." This confrontation between John and Herod was not just a casual disagreement; it was a bold and dangerous act of defiance against a powerful ruler who had the authority to imprison and execute him. John's courage in calling out Herod's sin, despite the potential consequences, speaks to the depth of his moral conviction. He could have remained silent or chosen to look the other way, but John knew that righteousness required him to speak the truth, no matter how uncomfortable or dangerous it might be. This unwavering commitment to the truth is one of the key reasons why John the Baptist was so great in the eyes of God.

Herod's reaction to John's rebuke is also telling. Although Herod had the power to imprison and ultimately execute John, the Bible indicates that Herod had a certain level of respect for John's character and message. In Mark 6:20, it says, "For Herod feared John, knowing that he was a just man and an holy, and observed him; and when he heard him, he did many things, and heard him gladly." This verse shows that even though Herod was living in sin and did not want to hear John's condemnation of his actions, he still recognized that John was a righteous and holy man. Herod's fear of John was not just a fear of the man himself, but a fear of the truth and moral authority that John represented. Despite Herod's personal acknowledgment of John's righteousness, he ultimately allowed himself to be swayed by Herodias, who harbored a deep grudge against John for exposing her unlawful marriage. Herodias was determined to silence John and saw an opportunity to do so during Herod's birthday celebration. Herodias's daughter, Salome, danced for Herod and his guests, and Herod, pleased with her performance, made a foolish and boastful promise, saying, "Ask of me whatsoever thou wilt, and I will give it thee" (Mark 6:22). Salome, at the prompting of her mother, asked for the head of John the Baptist on a platter. Herod, though grieved by the request, felt bound by his public promise and ordered John's execution.

John the Baptist's death was not just a tragic consequence of political intrigue or personal vendettas; it was the result of his steadfast refusal to compromise on his moral convictions. John knew that confronting Herod about his sin could lead to imprisonment or worse, but he stood firm in his commitment to righteousness. He valued the truth of God's law more than his own safety or comfort, and this willingness to stand for the truth, even in the face of death, is what made John truly great. Jesus Himself recognized John's greatness, declaring in Matthew 11:11, "Verily I say unto you, Among them that are born of women there hath not risen a greater than John the Baptist." This statement from Jesus highlights the unique and profound role that John played in God's plan, and it also underscores the significance of John's martyrdom. John's greatness was not defined by worldly success or power, but by his unwavering faithfulness to God's truth and his willingness to sacrifice everything, even his life, for the sake of righteousness.

John's martyrdom is significant not only because of the circumstances of his death but also because of what it represents in the broader context of God's Kingdom. John's life and death serve as a powerful reminder that standing for righteousness often comes at a great personal cost. Throughout the Bible, we see that those who choose to stand for God's truth are often misunderstood, persecuted, and even killed for their faith. John's willingness to face these consequences without backing down is a testament to his deep commitment to God's will. His martyrdom is a reflection of the reality that in God's Kingdom, true greatness is not measured by external success or popularity but by the depth of one's faith and the willingness to stand for what is right, even when it is costly. John's example challenges all believers to consider whether they are willing to stand for righteousness in their own lives, even when it means facing opposition or suffering.

Another important aspect of John's martyrdom is the way it foreshadows the ultimate sacrifice that Jesus Himself would make on the cross. John's role as the forerunner of Christ was not only to prepare the way for Jesus through his preaching of repentance but also to model the kind of sacrificial obedience that Jesus would embody in His own death. Just as John was willing to die for the truth, Jesus would later lay down His life for the salvation of the world. In this sense, John's martyrdom can be seen as a precursor to the greater sacrifice that Jesus would make. John's death reminds us that the path of righteousness often involves suffering, but it also points to the hope of resurrection and the ultimate victory of God's Kingdom. John's martyrdom was not the end of his story; it was the culmination of a life lived in faithful obedience to God, and it serves as a powerful example of what it means to live a life of true greatness in the eyes of God.

John's willingness to sacrifice his life for the sake of righteousness also highlights the importance of moral courage in the life of a believer. In a world where compromise and moral relativism are often the norm, John's example stands as a powerful testimony to the necessity of standing firm in one's convictions. John could have chosen to remain silent about Herod's sin, or he could have softened his message to avoid conflict, but he knew that righteousness demanded more. He understood that being faithful to God's truth required him to speak out, even when it was uncomfortable or dangerous. This moral courage is one of the key qualities that made John great, and it is a quality that all believers are called to emulate. John's life and death remind us that being a follower of Christ means standing for righteousness, even when it comes at a great personal cost.

In addition to his moral courage, John's martyrdom also highlights his deep humility and submission to God's will. Throughout his life, John consistently pointed people away from himself and toward Jesus, saying, "He must increase, but I must decrease" (John 3:30). John's willingness to step aside and let Jesus take center stage was a reflection of his deep understanding of his role in God's plan. He knew that his purpose was to prepare the way for the Messiah, and he was content to fade into the background once Jesus began His public ministry. This humility extended even to his death, as John never sought to preserve his own life or avoid the consequences of his actions. He fully trusted in God's plan, even when it meant laying down his life for the sake of righteousness. This humility is another key aspect of John's greatness, as it demonstrates his complete surrender to God's will and his deep faith in God's ultimate justice.

John's martyrdom also serves as a reminder of the eternal perspective that believers are called to have. While John's death may have seemed like a tragic and unjust end from a human perspective, it was, in fact, a victory in the eyes of God. John's willingness to die for the truth was a testimony to his faithfulness, and his reward was not in this life but in the life to come. Jesus' declaration of John's greatness in Matthew 11:11 affirms that John's sacrifice was not in vain. In God's Kingdom, those who are willing to lay down their lives for the sake of righteousness are considered great, and their reward is eternal. John's life and death challenge us to consider whether we are living with an eternal perspective, prioritizing God's truth and righteousness above our own comfort or safety. His martyrdom reminds us that true greatness is found not in preserving our lives but in giving them up for the sake of the gospel.

In conclusion, what made John the Baptist great was not just his role as the forerunner of Christ but also his willingness to become a martyr for righteousness. John's life was marked by a deep commitment to God's truth, a boldness in confronting sin, and a willingness to sacrifice everything for the sake of righteousness. His ultimate act of martyrdom was the culmination of a life lived in faithful obedience to God, and it serves as a powerful example of what it means to live a life of true greatness in the Kingdom of God. John's death was not the end of his story but a testimony to the power of moral courage, humility, and faithfulness. His willingness to stand firm in his convictions, even in the face of death, is a reminder that being a follower of Christ requires a willingness to suffer for the truth. John's life and death challenge us to live with an eternal perspective, prioritizing God's Kingdom above all else and being willing to stand for righteousness, no matter the cost. His martyrdom is a testament to the greatness that comes from living a life fully devoted to God's will, and it continues to inspire believers to this day.

Conclusion

In conclusion, "God's Chosen Herald: The Calling and Greatness of John the Baptist" leaves readers with a profound understanding of the singular role John played in God's redemptive plan and the extraordinary qualities that made him great in the eyes of Christ. As the forerunner to Jesus, John's life challenges us to consider the depth of our own faith and commitment to God's calling, no matter the personal cost. His unwavering dedication to proclaiming repentance, despite opposition and misunderstanding, exemplifies a life wholly surrendered to God's purpose. John's fearlessness in confronting sin—even in the face of powerful rulers like Herod—highlights the courage required to stand for righteousness in a world that often rejects truth. His humility, demonstrated in his willingness to step aside as Jesus took center stage, reminds us that true greatness is not found in seeking personal glory but in magnifying Christ. The book compels us to examine the strength of our own convictions, as John's martyrdom underscores the reality that following God's will may lead to suffering, yet it is in such sacrifice that one finds eternal significance. John the Baptist's legacy continues to challenge believers to live lives of bold faith, deep humility, and unwavering devotion to the gospel message. In a time when self-promotion and personal success are often prioritized, "God's Chosen Herald – The Calling and Greatness of John the Baptist" calls us back to the essential truth that true greatness is found in serving God faithfully and pointing others to Christ, no matter the circumstances. Through the example of John's life, this book serves as both a stirring reminder and a call to action, urging us to embrace our own roles as heralds of God's kingdom, faithfully proclaiming the message of salvation to a world in desperate need of it.

Don't miss out!

Visit the website below and you can sign up to receive emails whenever Joshua Rhoades publishes a new book. There's no charge and no obligation.

https://books2read.com/r/B-A-AJLBB-JNEBF

BOOKS2READ

Connecting independent readers to independent writers.

Did you love *The Calling and Greatness of John the Baptist*? Then you should read *Why Did Jesus Weep?*[1] by Joshua Rhoades!

[2]

In John 11, we witness one of the most emotional moments in Jesus' ministry—His weeping at the tomb of Lazarus. This act raises a profound question: Why Did Jesus Weep? Was it a mere reaction to the sorrow around Him, or was there a deeper meaning to His tears? This book looks into that very question, revealing Jesus' compassion and His divine response to human suffering. His tears were not just for Lazarus but for all of humanity, showing us that Jesus is intimately involved in our pain.

His weeping wasn't a fleeting response but a reflection of His deep empathy and love for a broken world. Through lessons like "Death's Devastation" and "The Desire for Restoration," this book uncovers how His tears mirror His heart for us, offering comfort in times of loss and struggle. Jesus' tears weren't a sign of weakness but a declaration of His divine purpose. Following His tears, He raised Lazarus from the dead, foreshadowing His own resurrection and triumph over sin and death.

---

1. https://books2read.com/u/bPnNEd

2. https://books2read.com/u/bPnNEd

For believers, the question Why Did Jesus Weep? is a call to trust in Jesus' power, love, and promises, even amidst suffering. His tears invite us to embrace His compassion and extend it to others, offering hope in a hurting world. This book reminds us that Jesus' weeping was not just an emotional moment but a message of hope and restoration for all who follow Him.